GYM RATS:

MOVING UP

GYM RATS:

MOVING UP

MARY REISS FARIAS

Janet Venné, Illustrator

IrisBlu
publishing

Tucson, Arizona
IrisBluPublishing.com

This book is a work of fiction. Names, characters, places and incidents are products of the author's imagination or are used fictitiously. Any resemblance to actual events or locales or persons, alive or deceased, is entirely incidental.

First printing 2014

ISBN 978-0-9843406-4-4

ATTENTION BOOSTER CLUBS: Fundraising opportunities for your booster club are available! For more information, please contact IrisBluPublishing, www.IrisBluPublishing.com.

For Morgan

A special thanks to Marcy Schreiner for all the memories.

INTRODUCTION

Welcome to the third book in the *Gym Rats* series! If you'll remember, *Gym Rats: Basic Training* and *Toe Jam* are about best friends Morgan and Madison, and their adventures in the gym. The two girls can be found before practice making up routines in TGC's kids' waiting gym. Because the two of them can't get enough gymnastics, their coach, Deb, gives them nicknames: Madison is "Gym" and Morgan is "Rat." *Toe Jam* leaves off with Dakota deciding whether or not to join Morgan and Madison at TGC.

Moving Up continues the Gym Rats' story and takes on the same format as the first two books in the series. After Morgan and Madison's story, you will find the "Coach's Corner" and the "Drills to Skills" pages where technique and drills are discussed. I hope that you find these sections useful in the gym. Also, at the very end of the book is the glossary. While reading, you will come across certain words in **bold** print. These words are defined in the glossary.

My hope is that you've enjoyed the *Gym Rats* books so far and will like *Moving Up* just the same – or even more!

Thank you for reading!
    Mary Reiss Farias

Chapter 1

Moving Up?

I stood in the corner of the floor waiting for Amber to do her tumbling pass in front of me. I loved it when we got to "**cross tumble**." As Amber crossed the middle of the floor, I took a deep breath and started running. I hurdled and brought my arms straight up to my ears, reached for the floor, kicked my leg up over the top and did a round-off, back handspring, back handspring.

"Nice one, Morgan!" said Deb, my coach. "Now make sure you're keeping your feet together over the top."

"Okay," I answered as I trotted back to my place in line.

"Good job, Rat," said Madison.

"Thanks, Gym," I said.

Madison and I are best friends and on Pre Team together at TGC where we do gymnastics. We have nicknames; hers is "Gym" and mine is "Rat." Together, we're the "Gym Rats." Deb gave us the nicknames back when we were on developmental team because we *always* wanted to be in the gym, and every chance we got, we were!

Ever since I got my round-off back handspring, I'd been getting better and better at them. It didn't take me long to be able to do two back handsprings out of my round-off! Gym and I were learning a lot of new skills pretty fast. It was exciting to learn new things all the time!

After floor, it was time to condition. Today we conditioned with the level 4s and 5s. Deb and Coach Stephanie set up a bunch of mats in a line on the floor. We had to jump over and on top of them for 5 minutes without stopping. This was called "**plyometrics**."

I was first in line. I jumped on top of the first mat, then jumped down. I immediately rebounded and jumped over the second mat, then on top of the next. We continued to do this for a long time. By the end, my legs burned, sweat ran down my face, and I was tired!

While we stretched after conditioning, Deb came over to talk to us. "Girls, it's almost April, and it's time to decide who will be moving up to level 3 to compete in the fall. Now, we as a coaching staff will be doing skill assessments to see who we feel will be ready for competition in the fall."

"What's a skill assessment?" asked Leslie.

"It means we will be testing you to see what skills you have and what skills you need, much like we've been doing throughout Pre Team. There are set routines for level 3, so we have to see if you'll be ready to compete."

"When will we find out if we're moving up?" I asked eagerly.

"We will all know when the testing is over. Testing starts tomorrow," said Deb. "Now, you need to realize that it is not a punishment if you don't move up to level 3. Gymnastics is very individual and each gymnast gets skills at her own pace. I don't want you to be upset if you don't move up. The reason that we're doing things this way is because we want you all to be as successful as possible. We want you to be ready to compete when you go out on the floor in front of the judges."

My stomach flipped. *Judges!* If I competed, I would have to go out in front of *judges!* That was scary. But I didn't even know if I was going to compete. I hoped that I would be ready to move to level 3, but how was I to be sure?

When I got home I grabbed my favorite snack of lemon yogurt and wrote in the notebook I shared with Gym.

Dear Gym,

I'm so nervous! Do you think that we'll be able to move up to level 3?! I hope so. But who knows? I mean, how can we really be sure? Then – and this is REALLY bad – what if only one of us moves up? That would be TERRIBLE! I can't even think about it. AHHHHH!!!!!

If we both DO get moved up, then we have to COMPETE! In front of judges and everything. WOW. Allison says it's not that bad to get up and do routines in front of people. She actually likes competing, so she says. Maybe it will be fun? I'm excited to learn routines and then we would get a competition leotard too! We just have to be perfect in the gym to make sure that we get moved up. Who else do you think will move up? I'm sure Leslie and Amber will make it. As snotty as they are, they ARE good gymnasts. What about Dakota? I bet she'll move up too.

All right, I have to go to bed now.

C-U-L8-ER.

Rat

Chapter 2

CRAZY JACK

Jack was crazy. It was so hard for me to figure out what mood he was going to be in each day. Today my big brother was angry and sitting with his arms crossed, glaring out the window in the back seat next to me. Mom was driving my sister, Allison, to gym, and Jack and I had to go along.

I didn't mind going to the gym, of course. I'd go to the gym everyday if I could! In fact, Gym and I tried to go to open gym every Wednesday. We also got to the gym early whenever our practice started late. We made up routines in the kids' waiting gym. Right now we were making up a floor routine. We still had more to add:

M & M Floor Routine

- ☐ **Handstand forward roll**
- ☐ **Back Walkover**
- ☐ Run, Round-off Back Handspring, Back Handspring
- ☐ **Cartwheel**, step into splits
- ☐ Roll to **candlestick**, stand
- ☐ **Split leap**
- ☐ Pose

Jack's behavior was so unpredictable that my parents went to a bunch of different doctors to try and figure it out. They couldn't help him with much. They all wanted to put him on medicine to calm him down, but my parents didn't want to do that. So they kept searching.

"Crabby" Jack wasn't too bad, but when he was hyper, like he was the other day, that's when he really got annoying. My mom always looked worried, and my dad would yell at Jack to calm down. Nothing worked, really, until the day was over and he went to sleep.

My parents put him in pretty much every sport out there. He'd been playing soccer for a couple of years now, and they said he was pretty good at it; he could run hard, be aggressive, and kick the ball hard. I think my mom liked him playing soccer because it got out a lot of his energy and he was too tired to be hyper at home.

Since the doctors said they couldn't do anything for him except for putting him on medication, my mom started doing her own research. She told us that we might be changing the way we eat.

Chapter 3

LEVEL 9

"Bye," Allison said as she jumped out of the car with her gym bag.

Allison was finishing up her second **season** of level 8 and working to compete level 9 next season. She was actually pretty good – and I wasn't just saying that because she was my sister, either. She could do some really high-level skills. Right now she was working on her **Yurchenko** layout on vault; **front giants** on bars; back handspring **layout stepouts** and side **aerials** on beam; and **double fulls** and **front fulls** on floor! She really loved gymnastics (but I didn't know if she *loved* it as much as *I* did!), and she wanted to get a college **scholarship**. That meant that she wanted to compete gymnastics for a college and they would pay for her education.

Becca and Liz, the two level 10s at TGC, were already offered college scholarships. Becca still had 1 year left at TGC, but Liz was leaving in August for college to compete. That was pretty awesome! Gym and I wanted to get a college scholarship one day, too.

Al was so lucky because she got to work out with Becca and Liz all the time! Because Al already competed a season at level 8, she got to work a lot of level 9 skills. She was working out 20 hours a week!

Allison went into the locker room and put her gym bag and shoes in her locker. She heard Scott call her group, and she ran out to the gym.

For warm-up the group had to **sprint** on the **diagonals** on the floor and jog the edges. They didn't start by sprinting, though. They jogged three times through to warm up their bodies a little first.

Scott had them sprint the diagonals, but then he also had them do things like skips, **chassé**, run backwards, and **forward roll hops**. They went for 20 minutes and were sure tired and sweaty at the end!

After their long warm-up, the level 9/10s did a quick stretch and got right to their first event. Today it was floor. They spent the first 15 minutes working basic skills by doing a **complex**. All levels, including Pre Team, had different complexes for each event. The idea was that by doing the basic skills everyday, gymnasts would remind their muscles of the correct body position to be in. Then the correct body position becomes habit. This was called "**muscle memory**."

After their floor complex, the 9/10s worked on their own tumbling passes, trying to perfect them for the rest of this competition season.

It was March, so their State Meet was coming up in one week. If they did well there, they could qualify to the Regional Championships! Al didn't make it to Regionals last year, but she was competing really well this season. She really wanted to qualify!

The **compulsory** levels already had their competition season. It was during the fall. So now, during the spring, they worked on their skills they would **compete** next season.

We were doing that in Pre Team, too. Right now we were spending all our time on strength and working routines for level 3. And now our

skill assessments were tomorrow! I hoped I got
to move up.

Chapter 4

Don't Kill the Messenger

"Morgan, as soon as your dad and sister get home, we're having a family meeting," Mom said. "Go tell your brother."

"Why?" I asked.

"I've been doing a lot of research about the food we're eating, and we have to cut some things out," my mom explained.

"Like what?" I asked.

"That's what the meeting is about," answered my mom. "Now, go tell your brother."

I walked out of the kitchen and up the stairs. I wondered what foods my mom was going to cut out? We always ate whole-grain cereal and low-fat stuff like chicken and turkey. Mom made us eat salmon, which wasn't my favorite, but I could choke it down. "Man, I hope we don't have to eat more fish," I thought as I stood in front of Jack's door. He had put up a sign that read "knock at your own risk" on it. He was such a boy.

I knocked. "Jack? It's me," I said.

"'Me' who?" barked Jack.

"It's Morgan. Duh," I answered back.

"What do you want?" he demanded.

27

"Mom wanted me to tell you that as soon as Dad and Al get home from gym we're having a family meeting," I yelled through the door.

"That's stupid. What for?" Jack asked.

"Mom's going to change the way we eat."

"Yeah, right," Jack answered.

"That's what she said," I offered.

"She can say whatever she wants. I'll eat whatever I want," Jack retorted.

"Fine. I'm just here to tell you about the meeting," I said. I did a pivot turn with my arms in crown and left.

I hated talking to Jack. He was just so mean and unpleasant. Allison was much nicer as an older sibling. I don't know if it was because she was a gymnast too, or because she was a girl, or because she was just nicer. But every time I talked to Jack, I was never sure which Jack it would be. He was actually okay this time. I'm just glad he didn't open the door and beat up the messenger!

Chapter 5

CUT IT OUT

I was hand-washing my leotards when I heard Dad's truck pull up the driveway. "They're home," I said to myself. I finished wringing out my black and white flower leo and hung it in the bathtub. Mom made both Al and I hand-wash our own leotards. She said they were too delicate for the washing machine, and if we were in gymnastics, we could hand wash them ourselves! Our bathroom had leotards hanging all over the place.

I went downstairs and saw Mom giving Al a hug and telling her everything was okay. Dad just had a puzzled look on his face. Did she get hurt? What happened?

"What's wrong, Al?" I asked.

"Leave me alone," she answered.

So much for her being the nicer sibling.

"Go clean yourself up, Allison. We're about to have a family meeting," Mom said. "We'll talk about this afterward."

I followed Dad to the living room and sat on the floor in a straddle.

"What's wrong with Al?" I asked him.

"I actually don't have much of a clue," said Dad.

"What happened?" asked Mom as she walked into the living room.

"I really don't know," said Dad again. "I picked her up, we got into the car, I asked her how practice went, and she started crying. She wouldn't tell me what the problem was."

"You're sure she didn't get hurt?" Mom asked.

"No; I asked her that, and she told me that wasn't it," said Dad.

Just then, Allison walked into the living room. Mom and Dad stopped talking and we all watched her as she silently walked over to the overstuffed armchair and sat down, bringing her feet up to hug her knees. She just stared at the floor.

"Where's your brother?" asked Mom.

"He's coming," Al mumbled.

We heard Jack's feet skidding down the steps. He landed with a "BOOM!" on the landing. If we didn't hear that same sound multiple times everyday of our lives, maybe my parents would be concerned that Jack was hurt. But, no. That's just the way Jack descended the stairs.

"Sit down, Jack," Mom said as he walked in the doorway. He sat on the couch opposite my parents.

"What's this all about?" Jack asked.

"I'll do the talking," Mom said. "All you have to do is listen."

Mom talked. We all listened.

"All of you know that Jack has been to a lot of doctors, and none are able to help him. So, after a lot of research, I have been reading about diet and nutrition, and it seems that we really ought to make some changes," Mom began.

"Like what?" I asked.

"Well, for starters, we are going to eat *a lot* more fruits and vegetables. This whole concept of trying to eat one fruit or vegetable each meal isn't going to cut it. Our meals will be mostly made up of fruits and vegetables," explained

Mom. "In addition, we will be transitioning so that we will no longer eat processed foods, meat, eggs, milk, and cheese in the house."

"What?" demanded Jack. "What are we going to eat then?"

"We will be replacing all those things with a whole-food, plant-based diet of fruits, vegetables, whole grains, beans, nuts, and seeds," said Mom.

"We're going to be *vegetarian*?" asked Jack with astonishment.

"Technically," Mom said, "we're going to be *vegan*. But I prefer not to use that word. We're going to follow a whole-food, plant-based diet."

"What does "whole-food" mean?" I asked.

"It means that we're going to eat things that are made out of plants, and we're going to eat plants as close to their natural state as possible. For instance, instead of orange juice, we would eat an orange."

"That doesn't sound so bad," I said.

"Don't we need to eat meat for protein?" Jack was getting crazy-eyed.

"Nope," said Dad. "Plants have lots of protein in them – nuts and seeds, beans, and even dark leafy greens."

"Coach Deb says we need to eat protein after we work out to help repair our muscles," I said.

"She's right," said Mom. "You do need to eat protein after working out. A perfect snack afterwards would be carrots and hummus, or a rice cake with almond butter."

"What's hummus?" I asked.

"It's a dip made out of garbanzo beans. I'll make some this week so we can all try it," said Mom.

"Our plan is for us to make these changes gradually over a year so it won't be so difficult," said Dad.

"Like how?" I asked. My favorite snack was lemon yogurt. If we weren't going to be drinking milk and eating cheese anymore, we probably wouldn't be eating yogurt, either!

"Well, we're going to start with processed foods like most crackers, chips, cookies, cereals – anything with unnatural ingredients, preservatives and colors."

"Can I still have lemon yogurt?" I asked.

"Well, the kind of yogurt that we have been buying has artificial colors and flavors in it, so you won't be able to have that," Mom said.

"What can I eat instead?" I crabbed.

"I think that because we will eventually be cutting out dairy all together, we shouldn't find you another yogurt to eat. Instead, we should find you another plant-based alternative like hummus and veggies or beans and rice, or something like that. Most of what we'll be doing over the next year is taking out the things that are not healthy for us and replacing them with healthy, plant-based alternatives."

"We haven't heard from you yet, Allison. What do you think about all this?" asked Dad.

Al continued to stare at her spot on the floor and mumbled, "Whatever."

"All right. If you guys don't have any other questions, then for the next month we're cutting out all processed foods, and I'm not making any more meat for dinner," reminded Mom. "Al, stay here. Jack and Morgan, go up to your rooms and get ready for bed."

I looked at Al. She looked angry and miserable. Hopefully whatever was bothering her wasn't as bad as it seemed. As I left the room, I heard mom say, "What's wrong, Al?" I wished I could have been a fly on the wall.

Chapter 6

SKILL ASSESSMENTS NERVES

After I got ready for bed, I read what Gym had to say in the notebook:

Dear Rat,

I can't believe that our skill assessments are this week! I'm so nervous. Do you think that I'll move up even though I don't have my mill circle by myself yet? Man, I hope so. I REALLY want to compete this year! I wonder wha⁻ the tests are going to be like? Do you think that we'll be in a group, or will they do it individually? Ahh!! I have no idea what to think! I have to stop thinking about it – I'm going CRAZY!

I just need to go to stop thinking about it. See you at the skill assessments!

Gym

I was just as nervous as Gym to go to TGC in the afternoon. Tomorrow we were supposed to start skills tests. My plan was to write in the notebook on the way to school in the morning so I could get to bed early, but it wasn't working. All I could think about was how nervous I was for tomorrow. I turned on the lamp by my bed and wrote back to Gym in the notebook.

Dear Gym,

I can't sleep. Skill assessments are tomorrow, and it's all I can think about. I wonder what practice will be like? Will we even have practice? I have no idea if we'll be in a group or on our own. I hope we're in a group – I don't want to go through this without you. But then again, what if I fail? I don't want anyone to know it...

Uh oh – gotta go – my mom's coming!

Night – Rat

I slammed the notebook shut and turned off my lamp. As I covered myself back up, my mom came in my room.

"Morgan? Why are you still awake?" she asked.

"Hmm? Oh, I don't know," I said.

"Are you nervous about tomorrow?"

"A little," I fibbed.

"Just a little?" she asked with a smile.

I turned to her and started to cry. I couldn't help it, and I wasn't entirely sure why I was doing it, but I cried.

My mom gave me a hug and said, "You'll be okay, Kiddo. Why are you crying? Don't you want to get tested tomorrow?"

"Yeah, but I don't want to do bad," I said between sniffs.

"You won't do poorly. You will do the best you can do."

"What if that's not enough?" I sobbed.

"You can only do what you can do. If you aren't ready to compete yet, then you just aren't. All it means is that you need more time. One thing I've learned about gymnastics is that not everyone gets all of their skills at the same time. It takes some people longer, and if that's the case for you, then you'll have to deal with it – that's a part of competing too. But don't lie here and think the worst before you even go out there and try. It won't help. You have to know that you are going to go out there tomorrow and do exactly what you know how to do. They'll judge you on that."

"Okay," I said.

"You have to be confident. Every coach wants a confident competitor," Mom added.

"That's true," I said, wiping my eyes.

"Feel better?" she asked.

"I guess," I said.

"Take a deep breath and get some sleep. You have a big day tomorrow. And remember: you're not the only one going through this right now. Everyone on your team is in the same boat. They all feel the same way you do."

That was true. Even though it was hard for me to believe that Amber and Leslie were rattled, they *had* to be nervous for tomorrow. That made me feel a little better.

"Lay down," mom said as she pulled the covers up so I could get under them. "Sleep tight."

"Night, Mom. Thanks," I said.

"Love you, Honey."

Chapter 7

LUCKY PENNY

Despite my conversation with my mom the night before, I was still nervous in the morning. I had a good breakfast, though, and it was mom-approved! After last night's conversation about food, I kind of expected soupy oatmeal with some nuts on top for breakfast. Instead, my mom fixed a bowl of raw oatmeal with bananas, blueberries and strawberries. She topped it all off with a little bit of coconut water. I never had raw oatmeal before, and it was really good! And now that she's trying to help Jack, I looked in the trashcan and saw all of our cereals, crackers and chips in there. Farewell, my friends…

Meal one of day one was going well for me. Jack, on the other hand, would probably have some problems. He hardly ate fruits and vegetables because he said he didn't like them. But now that's really all mom's going to give him to eat. He used to eat chips and other junk food, but now mom has put her foot down. We'll see how crabby he is this week.

"You ready for today, Kiddo?" asked Mom.

"I think so," I said between bites of oatmeal. "I'm just going to do my best."

"That's right – you've got it," she winked at me.

Just then, Allison came down the stairs with a balloon and a card. "Here you go, Rat. This is for good luck today."

"Thanks, Al!" I said smiling.

Wow. That was a change since last night. I wonder what happened?

"You can read it in the car," Mom said. "We have to get going."

I brushed my teeth and grabbed my school bag and headed for the car. After I buckled myself in, I opened Al's card.

"Dear Rat,

Good luck today. I know you'll do great. And don't be too nervous. Here's a secret: The coaches make a big deal out of skill assessments because they want to see who will do well under pressure and who won't. It's like a test to see if you'll do well in competition. You're going to be just fine. Just slow down and think about how to do each skill. You can do it!
Love,
Al"

Taped inside the card was a penny. I picked it off the card. Underneath the penny, Al had written, "Lucky Penny." How cool; I had a good luck charm from my big sister. I loved Al!

Chapter 8

MORE NERVES

School took forever. All I could think about was skill assessments. I played different scenarios over in my head about how I would do on each event and how Deb would react after each one. I know I was driving myself crazy, but I couldn't stop.

Finally, school was out! I walked to my mom's car and got in.

"Hi, Hun," she said. "How was school?"

"Uh…I'm not really sure. All I could think about was gymnastics!"

"Morgan," Mom said. "You need to pay attention to your schoolwork."

"I know," I said. "I just couldn't help it."

Mom handed me a container filled with brown rice and black beans to eat on the way to the gym. She also had a big apple for me. I didn't mind this food. It was actually really good!

I finished eating just as we pulled up to the gym. "Have a good one, Kiddo," Mom said. "Oh, and here." She handed me the lucky penny from Allison.

"Thanks, Mom." I said. "I'll do my best."

"I know you will," smiled Mom. "Bye."

"Bye!"

In the locker room, I took my shoes off and put them in my locker with my gym bag. I took my time because I was *not* anxious to go out to the gym.

"Hey, Rat," Gym said behind me. She put her stuff in her locker.

"Hi," I said, handing her the notebook. "I wrote in the middle of the night last night because I couldn't sleep."

"I couldn't sleep, either," Gym said.

"Me either," said Dakota behind us.

"What do you have to worry about, Dakota?" asked Gym. "You're definitely moving up."

"How can you say that?" asked Dakota. "You know how bad my run is on vault."

"I think you're fine," I told her. What my mom said last night seemed right: we were all worried about skill assessments. I thought that Dakota would breeze in and be perfect. But she seemed just as nervous as the rest of us!

"Pre Team, let's go!" yelled Deb from the gym. We all walked in a clump from the locker room to the floor where Deb was standing with a clipboard.

"It looks so official," Gym whispered to me.

"It *is* official!" I said. "We find out if we're going to compete or not based on today!"

Chapter 9

Skill Assessments

"Girls, let's warm up," Coach Stephanie said. "Run 10 laps each direction around the floor."

We all got in a single-file line and jogged around the floor. No one talked. We were all nervous. No one wanted to blow it.

Deb led us through stretching while Coach Stephanie walked around with the clipboard. I'm not sure what she was writing down, but whatever it was, it made me nervous. And it seemed to make everyone else nervous, too. We all stood tall, looking straight ahead and doing exactly what we were told.

After we stretched, we started on vault.

"Girls, we're going to warm up with a couple of sprints, then let's see what you've got!" Deb said.

After our sprints, Deb gave us the order we were supposed to vault in. First up was Amber. She looked like a scared rabbit as she stood on the runway looking down at the springboard and **pit mat**. She ran, she jumped on the board, and did her **handstand flat back**. It wasn't a bad vault, but it wasn't as good as she normally does it.

I was next. I stood at my place on the runway, took a deep breath, and started running. I remembered all the **acceleration sprints** that we worked on as I sped up my run to the board. I jumped on the board and reached for the pit. I was going so fast that I went past a handstand and went to my back way too fast. Deb didn't say anything, but patted me on the back as I went back to wait for my other turn.

"Whoops," I said when I got back to Madison in line.

"Don't sweat it, Rat," she said. "It wasn't that bad."

"Deb patted me on the back on my way back here. What does that mean?"

"She always does that," Gym said.

"I know. I guess I'm just nervous," I said.

After vault we headed to bars. We had been working the level 3 routine for a couple of months now, and it was time to show Deb and

Coach Stephanie our skills. Dakota and Amber were really the only ones in our group that could do the bar routine consistently. I didn't always make my **front mill circle**, and Madison sometimes missed her **front hip circle**.

"Girls, we're going to do a quick warm-up of the bar routine, then we're going to go through one by one and watch routines," Deb instructed.

"Man, I hope I make my front hip circle today," Madison said. She looked nervous as she rubbed chalk on her hands and went to stand in line.

"You'll get it," I said.

"I hope so," she answered. "I'm just so nervous!"

"All right, Morgan. Let's see your **glide swing**, **pullover**," said Coach Stephanie. Deb was off to the side of the bars writing something on her clipboard.

I stood tall with my belly button pulled in, jumped, and then reached for the bar. As my feet went forward on my glide swing, my toes jammed into the floor stopping my swing all together.

"You've got to use your stomach and leg muscles to hold your feet up," Coach Stephanie said. "Keep going."

I stood back up and did my pullover. "Nice one, Rat," Deb said.

That made me feel better. At least I was doing *something* right. Hopefully Deb wrote *that* on her clipboard!

Once we finished warming up the routine, we all sat on the floor to watch each other. This made me *really* nervous!

"Madison, you're first!" Deb announced.

"You can do it, Gym," I said.

Madison gave me a half-hearted smile and chalked up. She stood on the panel mat in front of the bar and took a deep breath. Her glide swing went well, and she did a perfect pullover. Then it was time for her front hip circle. She pushed down on the bar, kept her chest up, and leaned forward, lifting her feet behind her. When she was upside down under the bar, she piked so that she circled around the bar back to a **front support**. She made it! The rest of her routine was a breeze.

We all clapped and cheered when she stuck her landing.

"Great routine, Madison!" said Deb.

"Awesome!" said Stephanie.

I gave her a high-five when she came back and sat down next to me. "That was so good, Gym! I've never seen you do a front hip circle so well."

"Thanks," smiled Gym.

I was last up on bars. "Morgan, you're up!" said Deb.

I stood on the mat staring at the bar. I really didn't want to repeat the glide swing I did in warm-ups. I took a deep breath and jumped. I caught the bar and squeezed my legs. I watched my toes as they glided over the floor and extended out at the end of my swing. I swung backwards and put my feet on the floor and immediately jumped into my pullover. My front hip circle went sailing around the bar. Next up was my **mill circle**. I did my **single-leg shoot through** and held my body above the bar before I switched my hands. I lifted myself up again, picked up my chest, and took a big step forward around the bar. My mill circle felt so easy! As I was coming up, though, I couldn't stop on top of the bar and accidentally did another mill circle. "Dang it!" I thought. I finished the rest of my routine.

When I landed my dismount, Stephanie gave me a high-five. "Nice routine, Morgan. Too much power on that one?"

"I guess so," I said.

"Good job, Rat," said Deb.

Why were they praising me so much? Didn't they notice that I screwed up?

Beam was next. It was nerve wracking. Balancing on four inches and doing a routine while everyone was watching wasn't easy. We warmed up and did our routines. Madison and Amber fell off on their **handstands**, and I had a huge wobble on my **split leap**. Dakota was still really nervous and fell off twice! But even with our screw-ups, Deb and Stephanie were really nice and seemed to think that we all did a good job.

After beam, we went to floor. This was fun. I liked doing my routine to music and tumbling hard. The hardest part for me was making sure I had straight legs on my **bridge kickover**. I squeezed them as hard as I could and it felt like I nailed it! My round-off back handspring, on the other hand, wasn't as good as normal. I tripped on my hurdle and did a horrible and crooked round-off. My back handspring had bent legs and my feet were apart. I finished my routine and walked off the floor with my head down. "I can't believe I screwed that up!" I thought.

The only one of us that did a perfect floor routine was Dakota. She looked like she had been competing the routine for years! "There is no way that I made it up to level 3," I thought to myself.

"Girls! Line up on the white line. We want to talk to you," Deb said.

We all walked as slowly over to the line as we did walking into the gym when practice started. I don't think anyone wanted to hear how poorly Deb and Stephanie thought we did.

"Overall good job, girls," said Deb. "There were a few jitters and nerves that affected your performance, but overall, I'm a bit impressed with how you did. Competition is a learning experience that happens over your gymnastics career, not something that you're just automatically good at. You all did some things today that you can learn from and try to improve on next time, right?"

We all said, "Yes."

"All right. Look happy! You should be proud of yourselves for getting through your first **mock meet**! Now go home, eat some healthy food, and when you come back tomorrow, you'll know the results of this, and then we will have the conditioning portion of our testing."

We turned and filed out of the gym. "That wasn't as bad as I thought," I said to Gym in the locker room. "Deb didn't seem to think that we did that bad."

"Yeah, but I didn't do great," said Gym.

"Neither did I, but we all did what we could," I answered. "Hopefully that was enough!"

Chapter 10

Surprise!

"How'd it go?" my mom asked when we came out to the lobby.

"Okay, I guess," I said.

"What did your coaches say?"

"They said that we did all right and that we'll do our conditioning testing tomorrow."

"That's great!" Mom said. "Are you glad it's over?"

"Yeah, but now I'm worried about tomorrow," I said.

"What if we keep your mind off of it with a sleepover with Madison?" offered Mom.

"Really? Okay! Let me go ask her!"

"No need," said Mom. "She's already coming home with us. Her mom and I wanted to surprise you."

"Thanks, Mom." This was good. Now Gym and I could suffer together while we waited for tomorrow. And maybe we would be able to find something to do to take our mind off of things!

Madison's mom came in the door with Madison's sleeping bag and overnight bag. "Hi, girls," she said. Madison and I went over to grab the bags out of her hands.

"Hi!" we both said together.

"Let's take Madison's things out to the car," my mom said. "You ready, girls?"

"Yes!" we both said together again. Madison said goodbye to her mom and we got in the car. All the way home we talked about skill assessments and replayed all the events for my mom.

We pulled into the driveway and my mom said, "Let's go get cleaned up and eat some dinner."

"Okay!" I said as we grabbed our stuff and jumped out of the car.

I walked into the house and went into the kitchen. Jack was in there trying to find a snack. "Argh! There's nothing to eat!" he griped. Mom walked in. "I have a headache," he told her.

"I'm sorry, Hun. That's probably because your body is getting used to not eating junk food. You used to eat a lot of it, and now you're eating none of it. You're doing a good job, and it'll get better soon. Dinner is almost ready."

"I don't want that gross food!" complained Jack.

"It's not gross; you'll like it, I promise," said Mom. "And here," she said, handing him a chewable pill. "Take some vitamin C. That will help your headache."

"Madison, why don't you take a shower first, then Morgan will take hers after you. Morgan, get a towel for your friend," instructed Mom. "Dinner will be ready when you get out."

After our showers, Mom called us. "Dinner time!"

"What are we having?" I asked.

"Brown rice with kale and garbanzos," said Mom. "With some other things on the side," she added.

"What are 'garbanzos'?" asked Gym.

"They're a type of bean," I told her. "We'll be eating a lot of them now."

"Why?" asked Gym.

"We are trying to eat more plants everyday," my mom answered. "I've read a lot of books about it, and I think it will help our family be healthier."

"Do they taste good?" asked Gym.

"See for yourself," Mom said, handing Madison a plate brimming with rice, bright green kale and garbanzos. My mom scooped up some tahini sauce and drizzled it over the top, then sprinkled everything with some sunflower seeds.

"It *looks* good," said Gym.

I know she finished that sentence in her mind, "but will it *taste* good?"

At the table were orange slices, tomatoes, cucumbers and bell peppers. "Take what you want," said Mom.

"Do you like it?" I asked Gym.

"Yeah, it's not bad," she said. "I really like the sauce."

I thought it was delicious. For some reason I really liked kale. And as much as Jack complained about not having anything to eat, he ate up everything on his plate and was already reaching for seconds. In fact, despite his headache, Jack was much nicer to us today.

Chapter 11

SLEEPOVER

After dinner, we went down to the carpeted basement where we had a beam and a big open space where we could practice our floor routine. Mom let us stay down there for a couple of hours before it was time to get ready for bed.

While we were brushing our teeth, I asked Gym, "Do you think we made it to team?"

"I have no idea," she said. "I guess it depends on how everyone else did, too, and how we do tomorrow."

"I wonder if they'll move everyone up?"

"I don't know. It wouldn't be fun to still be on Pre Team with a bunch of new kids," Gym said.

"No, not really," I answered. I really hadn't thought about that. That would *not* be fun. "Let's not think about it anymore. We'll find out tomorrow."

Gym and I talked for hours about everything. We both tried to avoid the subject of gymnastics, but it always seemed to come up.

"I wonder what it's like to compete," Gym said.

"Al said it's not really like practice, even though everyone says it is," I said.

"Hopefully we'll find out in the fall," Gym said.

"Lights out!" Mom called from the hallway. "Night, girls."

"Good night," we said in unison.

Even though we stopped talking, it took both of us a long time to fall asleep.

Chapter 12

AL'S DILEMMA

Allison's workout was ending just as ours was beginning. But when we got there, Al was sitting in the lobby with her gym bag, her shoes on, and was all ready to go. Her face was tear stained and she was scowling.

"What's going on, Allison?" asked Mom.

"I can't do it anymore," Allison cried into Mom's shoulder. "I won't go for my **series**, and I'll never be able to do it," she sobbed.

I stared at my sister then I looked wide-eyed at Gym. She was just staring at Al.

Scott came into the lobby. "She's going through a bit of a mental block, I'm afraid," he said. "She's physically capable of performing her series, she just won't go."

"What's the problem, Allison? Did you get hurt?" Mom asked, looking into her eyes.

"No," Allison answered.

"This happens sometimes," Scott explained. "Gymnasts work so much based on muscle memory that their brain shuts off, like autopilot. When the brain kicks in and the gymnast starts thinking again, her brain cannot comprehend the complexity of the skill."

"So this is normal?" Mom asked Scott.

"Unfortunately, yes. And more unfortunately, it's the week before State," answered Scott.

Al let out a loud sniff. "Let's go," Mom said. "Bye girls. Good luck today!"

In the car, Al all of a sudden started to cry harder.

"Allison," Mom said, "what's wrong?"

"You *know* what's wrong!" Al sobbed back.

"Okay, but why are you crying so hard?" Mom was perplexed.

"I don't know. I was just thinking about it. It's all I think about. And I don't *want* to think about it anymore!"

Chapter 13

CONDITIONING TESTING

"Pre Team! Let's go!" Deb yelled.

I couldn't help but wonder what was going on with Al. She competed her series in 5 meets already. She seemed fine the other day when she gave me my lucky penny, and she seemed fine when she left for the gym yesterday. But after practice yesterday and for the rest of the day she was not fine at all and talking about *never* doing her series!

"Girls, do 150 jump ropes each way. Then we'll stretch, talk about yesterday, and do our conditioning testing."

We finished our jump ropes then walked over to get a drink. "Hurry up, girls! Let's get stretching!" called Deb.

We made our way back to the floor. While we stretched, Deb explained the conditioning portion of the testing.

"You all did a good job on the skills testing despite some small errors. But we all feel that those problems can be overcome before the competition season, so long as your conditioning testing is up to our expectations."

"You mean it all hinges on today?" I asked with disbelief.

"Not really," explained Deb. "You all passed your skill assessments. I expect that you will probably pass your conditioning requirements, too, but we have to make sure that you will be strong enough to work through a competition season, as well as work on skills for level 4."

I wasn't convinced. I shot a worried look over to Gym. She looked worried too. In fact, *everyone* looked worried.

"Let's go!" yelled Deb. "On your feet! We're starting with leg lifts."

Our group walked over to the stall bars. "Legs need to be straight and toes must touch the bar in order for each one to count. You can keep trying until you can't do them anymore, but to pass you need 5."

Although we had all done this so many times in practice, it was nerve wracking having everyone stand around and stare while we did leg lifts, pull-ups, rope climb, and push-ups.

Chapter 14

Moving Up

We spent the entire practice doing our conditioning testing, and then we did a lot of flexibility. At the end of practice, Deb sat us down and recapped the day.

"Girls, you did a great job. You have worked hard since our last round of testing and have gotten so much stronger! I'm happy to say that you all will be competing level 3 next season."

We all cheered! We were staying together and we were going to *compete*! I looked at Gym and we both smiled and breathed a sigh of relief. We did it!

"We'll be having a meeting with you and your parents to let you know what you should expect as a member of TGC's team. Now, go home and eat a healthy dinner. And, girls, congratulations!"

Chapter 15

COMPLETE SHOCK

After practice, Mom picked me up. "Well? What happened?" she asked.

"I made it! We *all* made it!"

"Nice job, Morgan. I knew you could do it! I'm very happy for you."

"Thanks, Mom," I said. "I can't believe I finally made it to team! Now both Al and I are competing!"

"Morgan, I need to tell you something about Allison," said Mom.

"What's wrong with her?" I asked. "She seemed pretty upset."

"Well, she's having a hard time. She's afraid of her series on beam, and she's convinced that she will never be able to do it," explained Mom.

"She'll do it," I said.

"I'm afraid it's not that easy, Morgan. She's talking about quitting after the state meet next weekend."

"What?!" I yelled. "She can't quit. She loves gymnastics!" I couldn't believe it. There's no way that Al could quit. She's supposed to be in it forever! She's supposed to get a college scholarship and pave the way for her little sister!

"Shhh. Not so loud, Morgan. I know it's shocking, but she's really upset about this. Scott and I talked to her and we all have agreed that before she makes any decisions, she needs to have some private lessons to try to overcome her fear."

"Wow," I said. I was in shock. I just got onto team, and my sister might quit gymnastics. This couldn't be!

Chapter 16

TOUCHY SUBJECT

I didn't know how to talk to Allison after practice. I was so excited to be moving up to team, but she was so sad about what was going on with her. I didn't want to rub in the fact that I was doing really well in the gym and she wasn't, so I just didn't say anything.

At dinner, Mom said, "Morgan has some good news."

"What is it, Sweetheart?" Dad asked.

I looked at my dad. He was eager to find out my news.

"Go ahead, tell them," Mom said.

I looked at Al. She was just staring at her salad.

"Well, I made it to level 3!" I said. I couldn't help it; I was smiling from ear to ear.

"Way to go, Kid!" Dad cheered.

"That's pretty good," Jack said. Coming from Jack, I'd say *that* was pretty good.

"Good job, Rat," Al forced a smile. "I knew you could do it."

"Thanks, Al. Now we'll both be competing!" I blurted out. Allison looked over at me. My eyes opened wide. Why do I have such a big mouth?

"Yep. We're both competing," Al said quietly.

Chapter 17

ANOTHER
SURPRISE

Over the next week, Allison had private lessons with Scott after school to get her to go for her series. She didn't want anyone to watch her, so Mom or Dad dropped her off and picked her up an hour later. Even though I was dying to know if she was going for her series, I didn't dare ask her how it was going. In the car when Mom asked her how she was doing, she would just say, "Fine."

In my practices throughout the week, we all worked hard on the level 3 skills and routines. Coach Deb and Stephanie told us all about **deductions** and exactly what the judges would be looking for. They looked for *a lot*!

By Friday before practice, Mom was evidently going as crazy as I was, and finally demanded Al to tell her if she was going for her series or not.

All Al said was, "You can come and watch practice today. We're doing a **meet run-through** and will be finished early."

"I'll be there," Mom said.

I was excited to watch the meet run-though, too. When the competitive teams have a meet run-through before a big meet like State, the whole gym stops and watches their routines. Now *that* was pressure!

The **optionals** started on vault. All of them did really well. I can't wait to go to the meet and cheer them on! Their bar routines went equally well.

When it came time for them to do their beam routines, I started to get a little nervous. I saw Mom and Dad watching through the lobby window. Jack was even there to watch. A few girls went before Allison. Finally she was up. She saluted. She stood at the end of the beam for her **mount**. I saw her take a deep breath, and she started. She mounted the beam and danced her way up to the end of the beam for her series. Back handspring, back handspring. Stick. She did it! She went for her series and it was awesome! She kept going though her routine and stuck it. Phew! She was back – just in time for State!

I saw Mom and Dad high-five each other in the lobby and give Al a thumbs up through the window.

Allison looked relieved as Scott gave her a high-five and said, "Nice job!"

Chapter 18

STATE MEET

It was quite a drive to the State Meet, and it started early on Saturday morning. The plan was to leave after practice and get some dinner, then drive there and stay in a hotel for the night so Al could get enough sleep.

Mom handed Al and me our bags. "Your clothes are in here," she said. "Great job, Allison. We're so proud of you!"

"Thanks," Al smiled.

Scott came out of the gym. "Not bad, eh? She's come a long way since last week. Her confidence level is through the roof now!"

"She looked good out there," Dad said.

"She sure did," agreed Mom. "Go change, girls. We need to get going."

"Thanks so much for working with her, Scott. We really appreciate it."

"She was just as confused as the rest of us as to why she wasn't going for it," said Scott. "We just had to step back and reset her brain, which is much easier to do during a private lesson than during regular practice."

"Well, it looks like it worked. So thank you."

"It was my pleasure," answered Scott.

Al and I came out of the locker room. "You guys have a safe trip and we'll see you tomorrow morning. Eat and sleep well!"

We went to a local Mediterranean restaurant for dinner. There were a lot of choices for us. We started by ordering pita bread and hummus. I really liked the big olives that came with it. Mom ordered a big salad for all of us to share, and then we all had our own entrees. I had brown rice, lentils and broccoli. Fresh fruit came on the side.

We all had a nice family dinner together. Allison was back to her old self, Jack was actually being quiet and nice, and I was still riding on cloud nine from moving up to level 3. I couldn't wait to watch Al at State tomorrow! Now I could safely say that *both* of us would be competing!

On the way to the hotel, I wrote to Gym in the notebook.

Dear Gym,

We are on the way to State to watch Al and the rest of the optionals compete! I'm so excited to watch them. I know they'll do great. They did awesome in their meet run-through at the gym.

I hope I never go through what Al did this week with her series. She was so upset and thinking about quitting gymnastics altogether! I could never think about quitting. I mean, we're just getting started! Let's promise never to quit. All right, my dad wants me to turn off the light now. I'll talk to you later. I'll write after the meet and let you know everything that happens!

RAT

Coach's Corner

Hello, Coach Scott here. As you read, Allison had trouble with her series on beam. There was no physical reason for her not to go for the skill; her body just wouldn't go. Unfortunately, this is something very common for gymnasts to go through as they progress with their training. Sometimes it happens early on with skills, say in level 3, and sometimes it happens like it did for Allison, in level 9. It really can happen at any time during a gymnast's career, and it can happen more than once.

There are a couple of ways to handle this type of situation. More often than not, it will take some one-on-one time in the gym with your coach – and your coach will have to be at least a little bit understanding of your mental block. Here's how we handled Allison's series problem.

Mental Imagery – visualize yourself perfoming the skill correctly over and over again.

- It may be difficult for you to picture yourself doing it right away. Keep trying. Once you see yourself doing it, repeat it many, many times. Do this throughout the day and before bed.

- You may not be able to do the skill right away after you picture yourself doing it. In fact, you may have to perform this mental gymnastics for a week or more before you can perform the skill physically. But it is important for you to continue to watch yourself performing the skill.

- At some point while doing this mental gymnastics, you will feel nervous. Maybe your palms will sweat, as though you're being asked to physically perform the skill. This is good! It gets you ready for the real thing.

- While you're visualizing, you may get a strong urge to "go for it" at your next practice. This is great! 90% of the battle in a mental block is for you to decide that you are going to do the skill and that you're ready to do it!

Surround yourself with positive thoughts.

- You may want to read books on how to think positively.

- Find different inspirational quotes and think about how they pertain to your mental block.

- Replace negatives with positives. For instance, rather than saying, "Don't fall, don't fall, don't fall," fill your head with what it will take for you not to fall. What is it that you have to do to be successful? If you're performing a cartwheel on beam, you might want to try thinking, "high kick, lunge, lever, cartwheel, lever lunge, square hips, finish." If you fill your head with the things you need to focus on, there will be no room for the negatives.

It will be frustrating when you hit a mental block or fear, but it is so very important for you as a gymnast, and as a human being, to learn how to work through it without giving up. Find what works for you. Ask your coach for help. If it is something that you just can't seem to get through, there are many sports psychologists out there that may be able to help.

DRILLS TO SKILLS

Here are a couple of drills for a good handstand flat back, and a strong vault overall:

Running Drills:

These drills should be done the length of the vault runway.

- March on high toe. Depending on your strength, your hands can stay on your hips, or you can use strong "running arms" in **opposition**.

- March and slide your support foot back as you bring your front knee up.

- Run with high knees. You should perform this with your hands on your hips until you are in full control of your body. Then you can straighten your arms out in front of your body and hold them there while you run.

- Run kicking your bottom. Use the same arms as on the high knees drill.

- High skips, arms in opposition.
- Run backwards. Try to make your backwards run exactly the same as your forward run, just in reverse.
- Timed sprints. Have your coach time your sprint from the end of the runway to the vault.

Springboard Drills:

- What you need: a vault runway or floor, a springboard with a mat behind it.
- Run from about halfway down the runway.
- Jump on the board with your shoulders back on the board.
- Perform a stretch jump, stick and finish.
- The key to this drill is to keep your shoulders back on the board, keeping control on your stretch jump.
- Once you perfect the stretch jump, perform other jumps like tuck, straddle, etc. You may then move on to front tucks, with your coach's okay, of course.

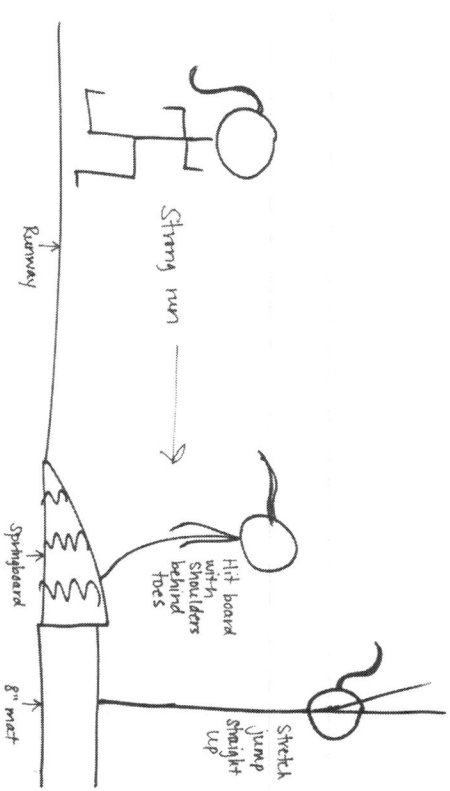

Runway

Strong run

Hit board with shoulders behind toes

Springboard

8" mat

Stretch jump straight up

101

GLOSSARY

8-incher: a mat that is eight inches thick

Acceleration Sprints: the type of run wanted on vault: begin slow, gain a medium speed in the middle of the runway, and increase to the fastest at the end of the run

Aerial: a cartwheel without hands

Back Handspring: a tumbling skill where you jump off two feet, arch backward to push off your hands and finish back on your feet

Back Walkover: a tumbling skill where you stand with one foot in front, arch back to the floor with your hands and walk your legs over back to a stand position

Bridge Kickover: a tumbling skill where you begin in a bridge position, then kick your leg over the top back to a stand position

Candlestick: a position where you lie down on your back and lift your legs straight up to the ceiling with your hips off the floor

Cartwheel: a tumbling skill where you place each one hand on the floor one at a time while at the same time kicking and straddling your legs over the top like a windmill, finishing on one foot at a time in a standing position

Compete: the act of performing your routines in front of a judge for a score

Compulsory: levels 3-5 in gymnastics where everyone competing performs the same routines

Complex: a series of basic skills used together to create a warm-up or workout for an event

Cross Tumble: performing tumbling passes using the diagonals of the floor

Crown: a dance position where you hold your arms gracefully above your head with rounded elbows

Deductions: the points taken off a routine in a competition

Diagonals: corner-to-corner on the floor

Double Full: a skill where you perform two twists in one flip

Forward Roll Hops: a conditioning skill where you perform a forward roll, jump immediately our of it, and dive immediately into a forward roll again

Front Full: a full-twisting front tuck

Front Giants: a giant swing around the bar with hands in undergrip, falling forward around the bar

Front Hip Circle: a bar skill where you begin in a front support, circle forward around the bar and end up in front support

Front Mill Circle: a bar skill where you split the bar and circle forward around the bar

Front Support: a position on bars or beam where you hold your body up with straight arms so that your thighs are resting on the apparatus

Glide Swing: a bar skill where you swing under the bar (the first part of a glide kip)

Handstand: a position where you stand vertically on your hands

Handstand Flat Back: a vault where after you jump on the board, you do a handstand and fall to your back in a tight body position (the level 3 competitive vault)

Handstand Forward Roll: a tumbling skill where you perform a handstand then roll forward out of it

Layout Step Out: a skill where you perform a back handspring step out with no hands

Leap: a dance skill where you take off of one foot and land on one foot

Meet Run-Through: a (usually) shortened practice where you and your team run through your routines, usually before a competition

Moct Meet: also known as a "critique meet" where you and your team perform your routines in front a a judge before the season officially starts for experience

Mount: the skill that gets you onto an apparatus

Muscle Memory: the way your muscles get used to doing skills by performing them over and over again

Opposition: a dance term in which the arm opposite of the leg you are leading with is in front

Optionals: the term used for levels 6-elite; those competitors that make up their own routines

Pit: a very thick cushiony mat, sometimes in-ground, sometimes above ground where level 3s perform their vault

Pivot Turn: a turn done on two feet when they are in relevé lock

Plyometrics: a conditioning circuit where you continually jump on top of and over blocks for a period of time

Pullover: a skill on bars where you begin in a hanging position (or on the floor under the low bar) and lift your hips to the bar and circle backwards around the bar until you finish in a front support

Round-off: a skill where you begin like a cartwheel, but you bring your feet together in the middle and land on two feet

Scholarship: an agreement between an athlete and a college to compete for the school in exchange for tuition

Season: the part of the year during which you compete

Series: a connection of two skills in a row; most often associated with an acro connection on beam

Single-leg Shoot Through: a bar skill where you cast and place one foot through your hands

Sprint: a short fast run, as on vault

Vegan: a diet where you do not eat any animal products

Vegetarian: a diet where you do not eat any meat

Yurchenko: a vault skill where you perform a round-off onto the springboard, a back handspring onto the vault table and a salto before landing on the floor (see *Gym Rats: Toe Jam* for more detailed information)

About the Author

The youngest of eleven children, Mary Reiss Farias grew up on a farm in Corcoran, Minnesota. At the age of five, she began gymnastics. Loving the sport, she continued at North Shore Gymnastics Association in Long Lake, Minnesota until she graduated from high school. Good grades and her level 10 skill set earned her a scholarship to the University of Arizona in Tucson where she competed all four years of her eligibility. Mary then spent the next decade coaching, among other occupations. In 2012, she and her husband, Marc, opened their own gymnastics training center in Tucson,

Arizona, called Tucson Gymnastics Center. Marc and Mary have one daughter. This is Mary's third book.

Other books by Mary Reiss Farias:

Gym Rats: Basic Training
Book 1 in the *Gym Rats* series

Read about Morgan as she goes through the highs and lows of going for her round-off back handspring for the first time! Meet her best friend, Madison, and be up close and personal as you read their notes to each other. Also, learn some great drills and techniques for your round-off back handspring from Morgan and Madison's coach, Deb. She even gives you the tricks to learning a high-level skill!

Gym Rats: Toe Jam
Book 2 in the *Gym Rats* series

Best friends and gymnasts, Morgan and Madison, continue their exploits in the second book of the fictional *Gym Rats* series. There isn't a gymnast in the world that hasn't gotten hurt and was unable to perform at her best. The Gym Rats get a taste of what injury is like in *Gym Rats: Toe Jam*.

Other projects by IrisBlu Publishing:

Home Fire: Sarah and Charlie by Nancy Ann
Book 1 in the *Home Fire* series

Home Fire: The Journey Home by Nancy Ann
Book 2 in the *Home Fire* series

Home Fire: The Big Year By Nancy Ann
Book 3 in the *Home Fire* Series (coming May 2014)

For teens and young adults, the *Home Fire* series follows Sarah as she moves to the woods of northern Minnesota. Be a part of her interesting journey as she meets many friends and obstacles along the way.

With All Due Respect

Do you know an older American with a great story? IrisBlu Publishing is collecting the stories of our older Americans to be published in magazine form. These stories should be written by Americans 70 years of age or older and should capture what life was like in the early decades of the 20th Century. For more imformation, please visit www.withalldduerespectproject.com.

Made in the USA
Middletown, DE
11 December 2022

18076841R00068